S0-BBJ-604

A Fair Land to Build In
The Architecture of the Empire State

A Fair Land to Build In
The Architecture of the Empire State

Brendan Gill

Preservation League of New York State

This catalogue is based on a film of the same
name written and narrated by Brendan Gill
for the Preservation League of New York State.

The Preservation League is a not-for-profit
organization whose primary purpose is to stimu-
late and encourage public participation in historic
preservation throughout New York State.

Preservation League of New York State
307 Hamilton Street
Albany, New York 12210
518-462-5658

Copyright © 1984 by the Preservation League
of New York State, Inc.

All Rights Reserved

First Edition

ISBN: 0-942000-04-8

Introduction

"A Fair Land to Build In: The Architecture of the Empire State" is a celebration of the buildings of New York State. The enterprise began in 1980 when the National Trust for Historic Preservation held its thirty-fourth annual conference in New York City. Eager that participants in the conference, coming from all over the country, should learn as much as possible about our New York architecture, the Preservation League undertook the production of a slide/tape program that, though not skimping the landmarks of New York City, would call attention to the exceptional profusion of building styles that have developed throughout the entire state over the past three centuries.

Beginning in the early summer of 1980, Preservation League trustees and staff set to work. Two professional photographers were commissioned to travel the length and breadth of the state. Simultaneously, scores of public and private slide collections were examined in order to identify photographs taken in every season from many angles of vision, whether at long range or close up. Over twenty-five thousand separate images of buildings and landscapes were scrutinized before six hundred of the most suitable slides were selected for assembling into a 30-minute, six-projector show. Our Chairman, Brendan Gill, composed and narrated the script. The project was directed by two consultants, the audio-visual designer Rusty Russell and John P. Grady, a partner at Chermayeff & Geismar Associates, who served as executive producer.

Following a premiere at the Waldorf-Astoria Hotel, on October 10, 1980, the program was converted to 16 mm. film and videotape. Since then it has entertained hundreds of audiences, including civic and business groups, historical and cultural agencies, and students; thousands of other viewers have seen the show on public television stations. Almost without exception, viewers have been captivated by the beauty and diversity of the architecture of New York State and challenged by a desire to know where the many structures in the show are located and when they were built. We are publishing this catalogue to record these images in a permanent form and to document the history and location of the nearly four hundred buildings featured in the film.

The Preservation League is indebted to the generosity of many individuals and institutions for the production of "A Fair Land to Build In," both as a visual program and as a catalogue.

We are especially grateful to Joan K. Davidson, President of The J. M. Kaplan Fund, who from the very beginning of the project offered her support and guidance.

The American Express Foundation, headed by Stephen S. Halsey, provided generous support for both the visual program and the book.

Other contributions were made by architect Philip Johnson, Mobil Foundation, Mohawk Paper Mills, our membership, and anonymous donors. Government funding was provided by the New York State Council on the Arts and the Office of Motion Picture and Television Development of the New York State Department of Commerce. The many individuals and agencies who generously lent slides are acknowledged on page 60. We are also happy to thank on page 56 the many property owners who welcomed our photographers and staff and made their task an agreeable one.

Diana S. Waite, Executive Director

What an extraordinary variety of architectural styles the buildings published in this catalogue display! The variety is thanks to differences in purpose, in location, in time of construction, and in the nature of the materials used; also, to differences in the culture of the builders. For over three centuries, great numbers of people have been pouring into a single comparatively limited area, bringing with them a welcome multiplicity of customs and convictions. It is a happy fact of architectural history that we build not only out of need but out of aspiration as well.

1. Flatiron Building
175 Fifth Avenue
New York
D.H. Burnham & Co., architects
1902

2. Residence
Tuxedo Park
c. 1900

3. Church
Clarksville

4. Highbridge Tower
West 173rd Street in
Highbridge Park
New York
John B. Jervis, architect (attrib.)
1872

5. Chenango County
Courthouse
North Broad and
West Main streets
Norwich
1839

6. Railroad crossing tower
Utica

7. Olana
Route 9G
Hudson
Frederic E. Church, architect,
with Calvert Vaux, consulting
architect
1870-74; 1888-90

8. Residence
Sackets Harbor
Barnabas Waterman, architect
(attrib.)
1808-15

9. Drawing room, Rokeby
River Road
Barrytown
Stanford White, architect
1895-96

10. Smoking room, Woodside
485 East Avenue
Rochester
Herter Brothers, decorators
c. 1890

1   2   3

4   5   6

7   8

9   10

11. Major's Inn
Marion Avenue and
Commercial Street
Gilbertsville
Augustus Nicholas Allen,
architect
1895-96

12. John E. Erdmann House
Lily Pond Lane
East Hampton
Albro & Lindeberg, architects
1912; 1927

13. Hannibal French House
Main Street
Sag Harbor
c. 1860

14. Conservatory Range
New York Botanical Garden
Bronx
William R. Cobb, architect,
for Lord & Burnham Co.
1899-1902

15. Cannon Tomb
Oakwood Cemetery
Troy
c. 1900

16. Gazebo
Mohonk Mountain House
Lake Mohonk near New Paltz

17. Montauk Club
25 Eighth Avenue
Brooklyn
Francis H. Kimball, architect
1891

18. Residence
New York

19. Munson-Williams-Proctor
Institute
310 Genesee Street
Utica
Philip Johnson, architect
1960

20. Haupt House
Amagansett
Gwathmey-Siegel & Associates,
architects
1976

21. Residence
Fishers Island
Edward Larrabee Barnes,
architect
1964

In an area slightly smaller than England or Greece, bold extremes of geography and climate are encountered. The land rises from sea level to mountains five thousand feet high. To the East, the view is of the Atlantic Ocean; to the West, of the Great Lakes. Two hundred inches of snow fall annually in one corner of the area; in another grow thick stands of semitropical bamboo. Beginning in the sixteenth century, the first Europeans reached America by water, and it was by water that they entered the continent and took possession of it. The earliest explorer of the region, Verrazano, perceived at once the importance of a certain harbor that he chanced to enter. In his ship's log, he wrote, " . . . we found a very pleasant situation among some steep hills, through which a very large river, deep at its mouth, forced its way to the sea . . ." Sailing up the river, later explorers sought a speedy northwest passage to the riches of the Orient. Though the river proved a disappointment in that respect, it became a major point of entry to the New World. "This is a very good land to fall in with," wrote Henry Hudson, "and a wonderfully fine country to see. . . . Never in my life have I set foot on such fertile soil, and it abounds in trees of many different kinds." The oldest mountains on earth lifted themselves above the river and the verdant lowlands. One range of the Appalachians, the Catskills, was singularly benign in aspect; the other, the Adirondacks, was fierce and inaccessible, and to this day some six million acres of it remain by law a wilderness.

11

12, 13

14

15, 16

17

18

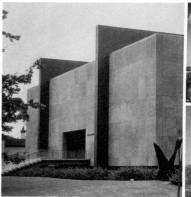

19

20, 21

22

23, 24

25   26

27   28

29   30

31   32

Where the river named for Henry Hudson empties into the Atlantic, it was natural for the early Dutch to set up a trading post, which, like Venice in the Old World, grew from a muddy fortified village on an obscure island to a mighty port and one of the most splendid cities on earth. Melville said of it that it was "belted round by wharves as Indian isles by coral reefs – commerce surrounds it with her surf." And with characteristic gusto Walt Whitman called it "the great place of the western continent, the heart, the brain, the focus, the mainspring, the pinnacle, the extremity, the no more beyond, of the New World."

22. Chapel and Crematorium
Mount Hope Cemetery
Rochester
Chapel: Andrew Jackson Warner,
architect (attrib.), 1863
Crematorium: J. Foster Warner,
architect, 1912

23. Kingston/Rondout 2
Lighthouse
Hudson River at Rondout Creek
Kingston
L.H. Bannon, builder
1913

24. Greek Temple
Untermyer Park
Warburton Avenue
and North Broadway
Yonkers
William Welles Bosworth,
landscape architect
c. 1920

25. Campbell-Whittlesey House
123 South Fitzhugh Street
Rochester
1835-36

26. Baron Steuben Plaza
Market Street at Centerway
Corning
Thomas, Martin & Kirkpatrick,
architects
1927-28

27. Bathroom, Olana
Route 9G
Hudson
c. 1890

28. Bathroom, Woodside
485 East Avenue
Rochester
Claude Bragdon, architect
1905-10

29. Sylvania
River Road
Barrytown
Charles A. Platt, architect
1905

30. Alfred E. Smith State
Office Building
Swan Street between State Street
and Washington Avenue
Albany
Sullivan W. Jones and
William Haugaard, architects
1927-30

31. Henry A. Deland House
991 South Main Street
Fairport
J.R. Thomas, architect (attrib.)
c. 1876

32. Gifford-Walker House
North Bergen Road
North Bergen
Aaron Gifford, builder
1870

33. Farm complex
Olana
Route 9G
Hudson
c. 1860-90

34. Church
Route 31
near Lakeport

35. "The Long Island Duckling"
("The Big Duck")
Flanders Road
Riverhead
Smith & Yeager, builders
c. 1931

36. Joab Center House
("Turtle House")
Route 9
Greenport Township
c. 1812-21

37. Darrow School Library
(Church Family Second
Meeting House, Mount
Lebanon Shaker Society)
Route 20
New Lebanon
1822-24

38. Cobblestone facade
Orleans County
c. 1840

39. Storage silos
Montgomery County

40. Hook Windmill
Main Street
East Hampton
Nathaniel Dominy V, builder
1806

41. Metal truss bridge
Gaines Basin Road
Gaines

42. Saratoga Race Track
Union Street
Saratoga Springs
begun 1864

43. Veterans' Room, Seventh
Regiment Armory
Park Avenue between
East 66th and 67th streets
New York
Louis Comfort Tiffany and
The Associated Artists with
Stanford White, decorators
1879-80

44. Kneses Tifereth Israel
Synagogue
King Street
Port Chester
Philip Johnson, architect
1956

33

34

35

36

37

38

39

40, 41

42

43

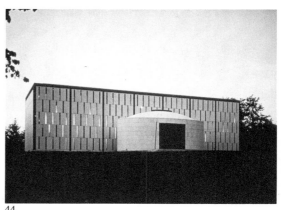

44

45

46

47

48

49

50

45. Richard Finucane House
168 Grosvenor Road
Rochester
Ward Wellington Ward,
architect
c. 1920

46. Residence
Oak Hill
c. 1820

47. Cultivated field
near Otisco Lake

48. Farmstead
Washington County

49. Indian Castle Church
Route 5S
Indian Castle
begun 1769

50. Iron fence
Hartford House
Route 39
Geneseo

By the time the British had routed the Dutch and named both the province and its chief city for a Duke of York, who was later to ascend the British throne as James II, settlers were moving steadily up the banks of the Hudson and its mighty tributary, the Mohawk. Before there were railroads and other means of overland transportation, the rivers and lakes of New York State served as the highways of commerce. When De Witt Clinton successfully completed the digging of the Erie Canal in 1825, the future pre-eminence of New York State was assured: the products of farm and factory moved easily and without interruption from the Great Lakes down to New York City and thence out into the world.

51. Japanese garden
Kykuit
Pocantico Hills
David H. Engle,
landscape architect
1962

52. Cultivated field
Marcellus

53. View from East River
New York

54. Brooklyn Bridge and
Manhattan Bridge
New York
Brooklyn Bridge: John A. and
Washington A. Roebling,
architects and engineers, 1883
Manhattan Bridge:
O.F. Nichols, engineer,
with Carrère & Hastings,
architects, 1909

55. Empire State Building
350 Fifth Avenue
New York
Shreve, Lamb & Harmon,
architects
1931

56. World Trade Center
Church Street
New York
Minoru Yamaski & Associates
and Emery Roth & Sons,
architects
1977

57. Chrysler Building
405 Lexington Avenue
New York
William Van Alen, architect
1930

58. Railroad bridge
near Mohawk River
Niskayuna

59. Erie Canal locks
Lockport

60. Erie Canal locks
Fort Hunter

61. Farmstead
Argyle

62. Number 3 Mill
("Mastodon Mill")
Harmony Manufacturing
Company
Cohoes
D.H. Van Auken, architect
1867-72

51

52

53

54

55 56 57

58

59 60

61 62

8

Water was as indispensable to manufacturing as it was to farming and commerce, since throughout much of the nineteenth century it was the only commonly available source of energy. Wherever rivers and streams could be dammed for power, mills and factories sprang up, and if they prospered, villages and towns accumulated around them and soon enough the towns grew into cities.

63. Stuyvesant Falls Mills
Stuyvesant Falls
1827; 1845; 1873-88

64-67. Dolge Company Factory
Dolgeville
1886-94

68. Number 3 Mill
("Mastodon Mill")
Harmony Manufacturing
Company
Cohoes
D.H. Van Auken, architect
1867-72

63

64

65, 66   67

68

69. Shaker agricultural buildings
Canaan

70. Outbuildings and doghouse
Rensselaer County

71. Burden Iron Company
Office Building
Polk Street
Troy
R.H. Robertson, architect
1881-82

72. W. & L.E. Gurley
Company Building
514 Fulton Street
Troy
Orrison Salisbury, builder
1862

The prosperity of New York State lured immigrants at first by the tens of thousands and then by the hundreds of thousands to seek jobs and homes within its boundaries. By early in the nineteenth century, it had become the most populous state in the nation, as well as the most important in respect to trade and manufacturing. Only Boston could rival New York City as a depot through which were funneled incessant waves of impoverished Irish immigrants during the 1840's and 1850's; other waves of immigrants arrived from Germany, Sicily, Sweden, Holland, Russia, and Poland. Many remained in New York City; others journeyed on to towns and cities to the north and west. Wherever they went, we can mark their progress by their ever-increasing impact on the culture around them. It was the case, for example, that the skills of the immigrant masons who helped to build the locks of the Erie Canal were later devoted to the construction of public buildings and costly private mansions; the traditions of the Old World were woven, in however modest a fashion, into the fabric of the New.

69

70

71

72

73   74

75   76

77   78

79

80

81   82

83

84   85

73. Syracuse Savings Bank
102 North Salina Street
Syracuse
Joseph Lyman Silsbee, architect
1876

74. Union Mill
Ballston Spa
N.R. Vanderburgh, architect;
R. Newton Brezee, architect
1850-86

75. First National Bank
35 State Street
Rochester
Mowbray & Uffinger, architects
1924

76. Case Building
82 St. Paul Street
Rochester
Louis P. Rodgers, architect
1882-83

77, 78. Statue of Liberty
Liberty Island
New York
Frédéric Auguste Bartholdi,
sculptor;
Gustave Eiffel, engineer;
Richard Morris Hunt, architect
1886

79. Ellis Island
New York Harbor
New York
Boring & Tilton, architects
1898

80. Oswego City Hall
West Oneida Street
Oswego
Horatio Nelson White, architect
1870

81. Residence
near Nedrow
c. 1840

82. Residence
Sharon Springs
c. 1850

83. Residence
Fonda
c. 1850

84. Ariaanje Coeymans House
Stone House Road
Coeymans
begun 1716

85. Abraham Hasbrouck House
Huguenot Street
New Paltz
1694-1712

86. Stone-Tolan House
2370 East Avenue
Brighton
Orringh Stone, builder
1792

87. Residence
Sackets Harbor
Barnabas Waterman,
architect (attrib.)
1808-15

88. James Vanderpoel House
("House of History")
Broad Street
Kinderhook
Barnabas Waterman,
architect (attrib.)
1816-20

89. Edgewater
Barrytown
Robert Mills, architect (attrib.);
additions by
Alexander Jackson Davis,
architect
c. 1820; c. 1850

90. Dining room, Edgewater
Barrytown
Robert Mills, architect (attrib.);
additions by
Alexander Jackson Davis,
architect
c. 1820; c. 1850

91. Residence
near Little Falls

92. Granger Homestead
295 North Main Street
Canandaigua
c. 1815

93. Residence
Dunnsville
c. 1840

94. Henry Rose House
Jerusalem
c. 1840

95. Residence
Auburn
c. 1840

86

87, 88   89

90   91

92

93

94

95

12

The successive transformations of the social structure of New York State can be traced decade after decade through its architecture. Some scholars assert that the closest the United States ever came to attaining Jefferson's dream of an agrarian republic was when the prosperous farmers of western New York were building their grand Greek Revival houses on every sightly hilltop. Working their fields by day, by night in their libraries they were reading Homer and Virgil in the original. The very place names of New York State reflect its lofty cultural ambitions: Rome, Troy, Ithaca, Corinth, Palmyra, and Athens all seek to summon up a classic past.

96. Parlor
Campbell-Whittlesey House
123 South Fitzhugh Street
Rochester
1835-36

97. Library, Rokeby
River Road
Barrytown
1858-59

98. Dining room
Campbell-Whittlesey House
123 South Fitzhugh Street
Rochester
1835-36

99. Staircase, Woodside
485 East Avenue
Rochester
Alfred M. Badger, builder
1838-40

100. Staircase, Rose Hill
Route 96A
Geneva
1837-39

101-105. Rose Hill
Route 96A
Geneva
1837-39

106. Hyde Hall
Glimmerglass State Park
Springfield
Philip Hooker, architect
1817-33

96   97

98

99   100

101   102

103   104, 105

106

107. Taft House
35 High Street
Lyons
Newell Taft, builder
c. 1850

108, 109. Brewster-Burke House
130 Spring Street
Rochester
1849

110. Residence
211 Main Street
Newfield

111. Carriage house
46 North Main Street
Homer
late 19th century

112. Residence
46 North Main Street
Homer
c. 1830; late 19th century

113. Delamater House
44 Montgomery Street
Rhinebeck
Alexander Jackson Davis,
architect
1844

114. Residence
Route 9H
Stuyvesant
c. 1840

115. Residence
2167 Fifth Avenue
Troy
c. 1860

116. Cazenovia Town Offices
Albany Street
Cazenovia
Alexander Jackson Davis,
architect (attrib.)
1847

117. Spirit House
Routes 26 and 80
Georgetown
Timothy Brown, builder
c. 1868

118, 119. Rokeby
River Road
Barrytown
1811-1815; 1858-59; 1895-96

Wood, being plentiful and easily shaped, has always been the commonest of building materials throughout the state. It lent itself readily to the Greek Revival style and, a few years later, to the Gothic Revival style as well. Two New Yorkers – Alexander Jackson Davis and Andrew Jackson Downing – did much to foster the popularity of the Gothic mode, which borrowed a make-believe medieval splendor from Walter Scott and other literary sources; this splendor was made manifest in stone for the well-to-do and in pine board-and-batten siding for the middle classes; whether in stone or wood, its charm did much to mitigate for our ancestors the harsh, money-grubbing aspects of the nineteenth century.

107

108, 109

110

111, 112

113

114

115   116   117

118   119

120

121

122

123

120. Lyndhurst
635 South Broadway
Tarrytown
Alexander Jackson Davis,
architect
1838; 1865

121. Timothy Copp House
Church and Joy streets
at East Avenue
Sinclairville
c. 1853

122. Ashcroft
112 Jay Street
Geneva
Calvert Vaux, architect
1862

123. "The Pink House"
Brooklyn Avenue
Wellsville

124. Munro House
Route 5
Elbridge
Thomas Atkins, architect
1851

125. District 5 Schoolhouse
Ridge Road
Childs
1849

126. Whipple House
Ridge Road
Gaines Township
c. 1840-50

127, 128. Cobblestone facades
c. 1840-50

129. Hawks House
Route 96
Phelps Township
1848

130. King House
Route 96
Phelps Township
c. 1840-50

131. Saunders House
Ridge Road
Gaines Township
1844

132. Cobblestone facade
c. 1840-50

133. Cobblestone Society
Museum
(First Universalist Church)
Ridge Road
Childs
1834

134. Residence
c. 1840-50

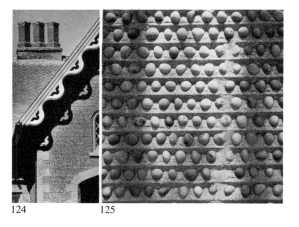
124   125

126

127, 128   129

130, 131   132

133

134

Some building materials go in and out of fashion in the course of a few years. Cobblestones are prevalent in central New York and were all the rage for a while, but they required far more time to lay than common brick, and as masons' wages went up cobblestone structures ceased to be built. Luckily, several hundred of them remain standing today.

For a short while in the 1870's and 1880's, an authentic American style emerged in our domestic architecture: big, rambling, shingled houses, with asymmetrical facades and open floor plans. Henry James complained of them that they had destroyed privacy in America; dolefully, he castigated the general absence of doors in American life. As the Greek Revival and Gothic Revival styles had been shouldered aside, so in its turn was the American vernacular style. The houses of the wealthy put on airs precisely as the owners of the houses did in dress and manner. "New" money made in railroads and stock-market manipulation far outstripped the "old" money possessed by the landed gentry. Businessmen and especially the wives of businessmen lusted to climb the social ladder and they succeeded in doing so partly by being as conspicuous as possible. They chose houses designed in mock-Tudor, mock-Spanish, mock-Colonial, and even mock-Swiss-Chalet styles – all permissible choices for clients who were seeking respectability in a mock-past peopled with mock-ancestors.

135. Residence
Loudonville Road
Loudonville
late 19th century

136. Sagamore Hill
Cove Neck Road
Oyster Bay
Lamb & Rich, architects
1884-85

137. Schuyler Quackenbush
House
Lee Avenue
East Hampton
Cyrus L.W. Eidlitz, architect
1898-99

138. Dining room
Richardson-Bates House
135 East Third Street
Oswego
Andrew Jackson Warner,
architect
1883-90

139. Library
Richardson-Bates House
135 East Third Street
Oswego
Andrew Jackson Warner,
architect
1883-90

135

136

137

138   139

140. Hall, Wickwire House
29 Tompkins Street
Cortland
Pierce & Bickford, architects
1912-13

141. Box Hill
Moriches Road
St. James
Stanford White, architect;
Lawrence Grant White, architect
begun 1892

142. Residence
Fulton

143. Residence
East Hampton

140

141

142

143

As a new and ramshackle aristocracy huffed and puffed its way upward, the middle classes, greatly increased in numbers, followed not far behind. New-fangled suburbs came into existence to cater to their needs and then more and more to their leisure. Golf and tennis were introduced. A fad word of the day was "park," which oddly enough indicated not that a certain parcel of land was open to the public but, on the contrary, that it was firmly closed to it. The very rich had Tuxedo Park, with its thousands of acres fenced against low-born intruders; the moderately rich had to fall back upon such moderately exclusive demesnes as Lawrence Park, in Bronxville, accessible on foot from the local railroad station.

144. Marymount School
1026 and 1027 Fifth Avenue
New York
Starrett & Van Vleck, architects
1903

145. Residence
New York

146, 147. The Jewish Museum
(Felix M. Warburg House)
1109 Fifth Avenue
New York
C.P.H. Gilbert, architect
1908

148. Parlor
Richardson-Bates House
135 East Third Street
Oswego
Andrew Jackson Warner,
architect
1850; 1867; 1883-90

149. Drawing room
Richardson-Bates House
135 East Third Street
Oswego
Andrew Jackson Warner,
architect
1850; 1867; 1883-90

150. Westbrook
Great River
Charles Haight, architect
1886-87

144

145

146

147

148

149

150

151. Residence
East Boulevard
Rochester

152. Vanderbilt Museum
and Planetarium
(William K. Vanderbilt II
House)
Centerport
Warren & Wetmore, architects
1910-36

153. Inisfada
North Hills
John P. Windrim, architect
1916-20

154. Olana
Route 9G
Hudson
Frederic E. Church, architect,
with Calvert Vaux,
consulting architect
1870-74; 1888-90

155. Sylvania
River Road
Barrytown
Charles A. Platt, architect
1905

156. Residence
Tuxedo Park

157, 158. Station Square
Forest Hills Gardens
Forest Hills
Grosvenor Atterbury, architect,
with Olmsted Brothers,
landscape architects
begun 1912

159. Larchmont Shore Club
(Jackson Gouraud Residence)
Larchmont
c. 1904

160, 161. Garden
Atkinson Allen House
32 Oliver Street
Rochester
Fletcher Steele,
landscape architect
begun 1916

162. Garden fountain
Tuxedo Park

151

152

153

154

155

156

157

158

159

160, 161

162

163

164

163. Garden
Atkinson Allen House
32 Oliver Street
Rochester
Fletcher Steele,
landscape architect
begun 1916

164. Casa Laura
Lawrence Park
Bronxville
1896

165. Will H. Low House
and Studio
Lawrence Park
Bronxville
William A. Bates, architect
c. 1890; 1898

165

166. Buffalo Savings Bank
545 Main Street
Buffalo
Green & Wicks, architects
1900-01

167. Buffalo State Hospital
400 Forest Avenue
Buffalo
H.H. Richardson, architect
1870-96

168. St. Paul's Episcopal
Cathedral
Church and Pearl streets
Buffalo
Richard Upjohn, architect;
Robert W. Gibson with
Cyrus K. Porter, architects
1849-51; 1870-71; 1888

169. Ellicott Square Building
295 Main Street
Buffalo
D.H. Burnham & Co., architects
1895-96

170-175. Darwin D. Martin
House
125 Jewett Parkway
Buffalo
Frank Lloyd Wright, architect
1904-06

In general, novelty was frowned upon, though some communities were willing to take exceptional chances. Buffalo, for example, grew rich because of its position on the Great Lakes; as the states of the Middle West opened up and prospered, so did Buffalo. Culturally, as well as economically, it was natural for Buffalo to look to pioneering Chicago and not to New York City for leadership. The radical young turn-of-the-century Chicago architect Frank Lloyd Wright was commissioned to design several highly individualistic buildings in Buffalo, including the delightful Darwin Martin house. And it was Wright's mentor, Louis Sullivan, who designed that robust and yet delicate masterpiece, the Prudential Building in Buffalo.

166

167

168

169

170

171, 172

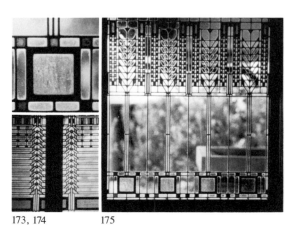

173, 174   175

22

176

177   178

179, 180   181

182

176. Darwin D. Martin House
125 Jewett Parkway
Buffalo
Frank Lloyd Wright, architect
1904-06

177-182. Prudential Building
(Guaranty Building)
28 Church Street
Buffalo
Adler & Sullivan, architects
1895-96

183. Mohonk Mountain House
Lake Mohonk
near New Paltz
Napoleon Le Brun & Sons,
architects;
James E. Ware, architect
begun 1859

184. Magnesia Springs Pavilion
Sharon Springs
L. Burger, architect
1863

185, 186. Sulphur Springs
Pavilion
Sharon Springs

187. George Washington
Denton House
Roslyn
1875

188. Vanderbilt Mansion
Hyde Park
McKim, Mead & White,
architects
1895-99

Once upon a time, Americans had been content to pass their summers as boarders in large mountaintop hotels, or as visitors to spas, taking the malodorous waters for their health, or as owners of simple wooden cottages; that vogue passed and was succeeded by a vogue for being every bit as grand in August as in January. A summer place might still be called a cottage, but increasingly it tended to resemble a castle; indeed, the Thousand Islands boasted several castles – great stone keeps, bristling with battlements, that leapt skyward off shelves of rock in the St. Lawrence River. On an island in the Hudson, Bannerman's Castle, the private arsenal of a munitions dealer, struck an appropriately Rhenish note. In the Adirondacks, a fifty-room structure with fifteen baths and a dozen encircling outbuildings would be called a camp, and how cozily one roughed it in that well-groomed wilderness, waited upon by a score of servants!

183

184

185, 186

187

188

189

190 191 192

189, 190. Boldt Castle
Alexandria Bay
Thousand Islands
Hewitt & Hewitt,
architects (attrib.)
c. 1896-1902

191. Gargoyle
Cherry Island
Thousand Islands

192. Boldt Castle
Alexandria Bay
Thousand Islands
Hewitt & Hewitt,
architects (attrib.)
c. 1896-1902

193. Bourne Castle
Dark Island
Thousand Islands

194. Bannerman's Castle
Pollapel Island
Fishkill
Francis Bannerman, architect
c. 1901-10

193

194

195. Kamp Kill Kare
Lake Kora
near Raquette Lake
William West Durant, architect;
Charles Hiscoe, architect;
John Russell Pope, architect
1898-1922

196. Stables, Kamp Kill Kare
Lake Kora
near Raquette Lake
John Russell Pope, architect
c. 1922

197. Uncas
Mohegan Lake
near Raquette Lake
William West Durant, architect
c. 1893-96

198. Camp Pine Knot
Raquette Lake
William West Durant, architect
c. 1876-1900

195

196 197, 198

199. Topridge
Keese Mills Road
Brighton Township
Theodore Blake, architect
begun 1923

200. Kamp Kill Kare
Lake Kora
near Raquette Lake
Charles Hiscoe, architect;
John Russell Pope, architect
c. 1917-18

199

200

201. Topridge
Keese Mills Road
Brighton Township
Theodore Blake, architect
begun 1923

202. Residence
Wainscott

203. Athenaeum Hotel
Chautauqua Institution
Chautauqua
c. 1881

204. Cottage
Chautauqua Institution
Chautauqua
c. 1890

Not everyone in New York State in the nineteenth century was bent upon taking holidays in great camps in the Adirondacks, or even in high-roofed bungalows along the seashore; many thousands of sober-minded citizens spent their vacations in a Chautauqua encampment, either at Lake Chautauqua itself or at one or another of its approved replicas, listening to lectures by distinguished speakers of the day. Chautauquas were entertainment with a lofty purpose; the other forms of entertainment available at the time remained suspect. Theatres, which often filled the upper floors of commercial buildings, dignified their existence by calling themselves opera houses and music halls. An implausible invention called moving pictures took a long time to gain respectability. By the twenties, movies had become the leading form of entertainment from coast to coast; in New York State, the glory of every Main Street was a movie palace holding many thousands of patrons and dazzling the eye with architecture on a scale of lavishness that rivaled Versailles.

201

202

203

204

205

206

207

208

209

210

211 212 213

205. Alumni Hall
Round Lake
Marcus F. Cummings,
architect (attrib.)
1884

206. Troy Savings Bank
and Music Hall
Second and State streets
Troy
George B. Post, architect
1870-75

207. Cohoes Music Hall
Remsen Street
Cohoes
Charles B. Nichols and
J.B. Halcott, architects
1874

208-212. Shea's Buffalo Theater
646 Main Street
Buffalo
C.W. and G.W. Rapp, architects
1926

213. Loew's Paradise Theater
2417 Grand Concourse
Bronx
John Eberson, architect
1929

214-218. Albright-Knox
Art Gallery
1285 Elmwood Avenue
Buffalo
Green & Wicks, architects;
Augustus Saint-Gaudens,
sculptor
1900-05

If the performing arts were often distrusted by our ancestors, the graphic and glyptic arts were not. Every sizable city aspired to support a museum with paintings and sculptures of an instructive nature. Even a naked female body in smooth white marble was considered edifying as long as it was said to illustrate some classic myth. As for public libraries, they, too, were an occasion for civic pride. In the eighteenth century, libraries were private institutions, owned by stockholders and run for their benefit; in the course of the nineteenth century, public libraries became an accepted responsibility of the community as a whole. Working in close cooperation with the public-school system, they helped not only to educate the native-born population but to Americanize an army of tongue-tied European newcomers as well. Public libraries and public schools provided the foundation upon which was to rise an elaborate superstructure of colleges and universities, and not alone for the higher education of men: the Emma Willard School in Troy, Wells College in Aurora, Vassar College in Poughkeepsie, and Barnard College in New York were all children of nineteenth-century enlightenment.

214

215   216

217

218

219

220

221   222

223   224

225   226

227

228, 229   230

231

219. *Esmeralda and the Goat*
Troy Public Library
Troy
A. Rosetti, sculptor
1867

220. Troy Public Library
100 Second Street
Troy
J. Stewart Barney, architect
1897

221. Windham Public Library
Windham
c. 1899

222. Akin Library
Quaker Hill
1898

223, 224. New York
Public Library
Fifth Avenue between
41st and 42nd streets
New York
Carrère & Hastings, architects
1911

225. Rochester Free Academy
13 South Fitzhugh Street
Rochester
Andrew Jackson Warner,
architect
1872

226. Coeymans Hollow School
Coeymans Hollow
Coeymans

227. School
Coxsackie

228-230. Acton Civill
Polytechnic Institute
Westerlo Street and Civill Avenue
Coeymans
Gilbert B. Croff,
architect (attrib.)
1873

231. New York State
Department of
Education Building
Washington Avenue between
Hawk and Swan streets
Albany
Henry Hornbostel, architect
1908-12

232, 233. New York State
Department of
Education Building
Washington Avenue between
Hawk and Swan streets
Albany
Henry Hornbostel, architect
1908-12

234. Crouse Memorial College
Syracuse University
Syracuse
Archimedes Russell, architect
1887-89

235. Nott Memorial
Union College
Schenectady
Edward Tuckerman Potter,
architect
1858-76

236. Emma Willard School
Troy
M.F. Cummings & Son,
architects
c. 1910

237. Smith Hall
Wells College
Aurora

238. New England Building
Vassar College
Poughkeepsie
York & Sawyer, architects
c. 1901

239. Emma Willard School
Troy
M.F. Cummings & Son,
architects
c. 1910

232   233

234   235

236

237, 238

239

In the heyday of railroading, every village and town in the state measured its
respect for itself by the size of its railroad station. The bigger the station,
the better the town – it was as simple and satisfactory as that. From the size
of the Union Station in Albany, completed in 1900, one would suppose that it
was intended to serve a city of a million or so; the fact is that Albany then
had a population of less than a hundred thousand people. New York City
boasted two colossal railroad stations, embracing hundreds of thousands of
cubic feet of empty air in a gesture intended to symbolize the might and
worth of the railroads that built them but that also symbolized corporate
vanity on an unprecedented scale.

240

241

242

243   244, 245

246

247

248

249

240. Railroad station
Fort Ticonderoga

241. Railroad station
Groveland

242. Railroad station
Syracuse

243-245. Union Station
321 Main Street
Utica
Stem & Fellheimer, architects
1914

246-248. Union Station
Broadway
Albany
Shepley, Rutan & Coolidge,
architects
1899-1900

249. Grand Central Terminal
42nd Street and Park Avenue
New York
Warren & Wetmore, architects
1903-13

31

250-252. Old County Hall
92 Franklin Street
Buffalo
Andrew Jackson Warner,
architect
1871-76

253-255. Albany City Hall
Eagle Street at Maiden Lane
Albany
H.H. Richardson, architect
1881

256. Oswego County
Courthouse
Oswego
Horatio Nelson White, architect
1860

Something like the same temptation afflicted government. Until the 1930's and the advent of the Great Depression, conspicuous display was admired, and public buildings took care to ape the opulence of the so-called private sector. The modest county courthouses and town halls of an earlier time, modeled after Greek and Roman temples, gave way to edifices immense in scale and ornate in their embellishment. City halls and federal post offices were nearly always grander than they needed to be for the bureaucratic purposes they served. They were overly ample and inefficient in their amplitude, but they were built to last; by an irony, their size and durability have made them ideal candidates for new public and private uses at the very moment when one might have expected them to be thrown down.

250

251   252

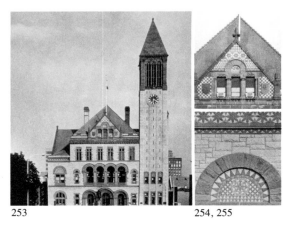

253   254, 255

256

257

258

259

260

 (261, 262 group)

261

262

263

264, 265

266

267

257. Seneca County Courthouse
complex at Ovid
("The Three Bears")
Ovid
Courthouse and
Old Clerk's Office:
O.B. and O.S. Latham,
architects
New Clerk's Office:
Horace H. Bennett, architect
c. 1845-60

258. Onondaga County
Courthouse
Montgomery, State and
Jefferson streets
Syracuse
Archimedes Russell, architect
1904-07

259. Surrogate's Court
(Hall of Records)
31 Chambers Street
New York
John R. Thomas, architect;
Horgan & Slattery, architects
1899-1911

260. Rensselaer County
Courthouse
Second and Congress streets
Troy
M.F. Cummings & Son,
architects
1894-98

261, 262. Municipal Building
1 Centre Street
New York
McKim, Mead & White,
architects
1914

263-265. Buffalo City Hall
Niagara Square
Buffalo
George J. Dietel and
John J. Wade with
Sullivan W. Jones, architects
1929-31

266. Third Monroe County
Courthouse
39 West Main Street
Rochester
J. Foster Warner, architect
1891-96

267. Tweed Courthouse
52 Chambers Street
New York
John Kellum, architect;
Leopold Eidlitz, architect
1858; c. 1880

33

268. Performing Arts Center
("The Egg")
Governor Nelson A. Rockefeller
Empire State Plaza
Albany
Wallace K. Harrison, architect
1965-78

269, 270. Governor Nelson A.
Rockefeller Empire State Plaza
Albany
Wallace K. Harrison, architect
1965-78

271-275. New York State Capitol
Albany
Thomas Fuller, architect;
H.H. Richardson, architect;
Leopold Eidlitz, architect;
Isaac G. Perry, architect
1867-99

As the capital of the state, Albany has received more than its share of architectural follies, and the ice-cold marble and glass fantasy of the Empire State Plaza isn't likely to be the last of them. Luckily, some of these follies, among them the Capitol building itself, are as splendid as they are bizarre. In the newly restored Senate Chamber, one feels underdressed because one is not in armor. Mounting the so-called "million-dollar staircase," who would wish it to have cost a penny less?

268

269

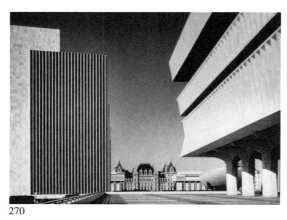

270

271

272

273, 274   275

276

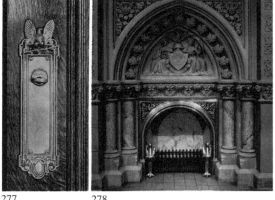

277   278

276, 277. Legislative Reference
Library
New York State Capitol
Albany
New York State Department
of Architecture, architects
1912-15

278. Assembly Chamber
New York State Capitol
Albany
Leopold Eidlitz, architect
1876-79

279-285. Senate Chamber
New York State Capitol
Albany
H.H. Richardson, architect
1881

286. Great Western Staircase
New York State Capitol
Albany
H.H. Richardson, architect;
Isaac G. Perry, architect
1883-97

279

280   281, 282

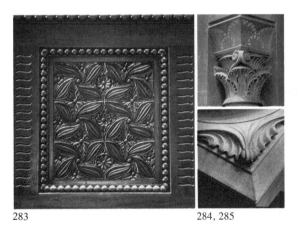

283   284, 285

286

287. Cast-iron building
361 Broadway
New York
W. Wheeler Smith, architect
1881

288. Cast-iron storehouse
(Building No. 38)
Watervliet Arsenal
Watervliet
Architectural Iron Works
(Daniel D. Badger,
superintendent)
1859

289. Gunther Building
469-475 Broome Street
New York
Griffith Thomas, architect
1873

290. Cast-iron storehouse
(Building No. 38)
Watervliet Arsenal
Watervliet
Architectural Iron Works
(Daniel D. Badger,
superintendent)
1859

291. Cast-iron building
New York

292. Cast-iron capital
New York

The fact is that American architecture, both public and private, has long coupled an aspiration to grandeur with an attempt to disguise a lowly purpose as a lofty one. A startling innovation in nineteenth-century architectural design was the prefabricated, cast-iron commercial building, pioneered by James Bogardus and others, which made possible the speedy construction of buildings that could be ordered out of a catalogue. Cast-iron plates were bolted together to provide a curtain-wall facade, supported by cast-iron pillars designed in imitation of ancient Greek and Roman pillars carved in stone. The greatest concentration of cast-iron buildings is to be found in New York City, in the historic landmarks district commonly known as SoHo, but many other specimens can be observed throughout the state. Cast iron proved to be less fireproof than its champions had proclaimed, and the vogue for cast-iron buildings in all their classic grandeur soon passed, but they served to open the door to the development of the steel-framed building and so, eventually, to the skyscraper.

287

288

289   290

291   292

293

294

293. Cast-iron building
New York

294. Haughwout Building
488 Broadway
New York
John P. Gaynor, architect
1856

295. Powers Building
16 West Main Street
Rochester
Andrew Jackson Warner,
architect
1865-91

295

296. DeVinne Press Building
399 Lafayette Street
New York
Babb, Cook & Willard,
architects
1885

297. Ilium Building
Fulton and Fourth streets
Troy
M.F. Cummings & Son,
architects
1904

298. Masonry building
New York

299. James Drake Building
Market Street
Corning
Pierce & Bickford, architects
1894

300. Bayard-Condict Building
65 Bleecker Street
New York
Louis Sullivan, architect
1897-99

Buildings with masonry bearing walls become awkwardly thick at the base if they reach a height of more than ten or fifteen stories; buildings with skeleton frames of steel are able to attain any height, their curtain walls of brick, terra cotta, and the like being no thicker on the ground floor than on the fiftieth. The Flatiron Building, once described as "an ocean steamer with all Broadway in tow," is an early high-rise made possible by the steel frame; somewhat later is the Woolworth Building, for many years the highest building on earth; it is the romantic ideal of the skyscraper form, rivaled only by the Chrysler Building and the Empire State Building. After these true towers came the inexpressive slab, which shoulders the sky but never scrapes it. For a time, a curtain wall almost entirely of glass became the fashion; lately, thanks to the need to conserve energy, architects have been returning to curtain walls that are easier to protect against extremes of heat and cold. Even sealed windows are beginning to be looked on with suspicion; young architects speak with excitement of "operable windows," which are nothing more or less than windows capable of being opened and shut.

296

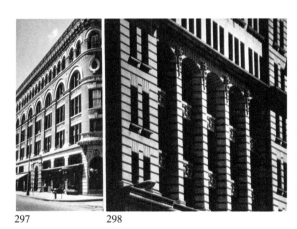

297   298

299

300

301

302

303

304

305

306

307

308

309

310

311

312

301-303 Flatiron Building
175 Fifth Avenue
New York
D.H. Burnham & Co., architects
1902

304, 305. Woolworth Building
233 Broadway
New York
Cass Gilbert, architect
1913

306. Chrysler Building
405 Lexington Avenue
New York
William Van Alen, architect
1930

307. Empire State Building
350 Fifth Avenue
New York
Shreve, Lamb & Harmon,
architects
1931

308. Office buildings
New York

309. Citicorp Center
Lexington to Third avenues and
53rd to 54th streets
New York
Hugh Stubbins & Associates,
architects
1977

310. Seagram Building
375 Park Avenue
New York
Ludwig Mies van der Rohe and
Philip Johnson, architects
1958

311. Lever House
390 Park Avenue
New York
Skidmore, Owings & Merrill
(Gordon Bunshaft, partner
in charge), architects
1952

312. Operable windows
New York

313-315. Consolidated Edison plant
Eleventh to Twelfth avenues
and 58th to 59th streets
New York
McKim, Mead & White,
architects
1904

316, 317. U.S. Custom House
Bowling Green
New York
Cass Gilbert, architect
1907

In earlier times, the need to mask a humble purpose by monumentality led to such structures as an enormous Renaissance palazzo by McKim, Mead & White, on Eleventh Avenue in New York City, which contains nothing nobler than a subway power station. Similarly, the U.S. Custom House, on Bowling Green in New York City, looks worthy to house the most puissant of gods, but all that has ever been worshipped there is money. In contemporary times, the mask of grandeur is quickly seen through; the white domino of a building that stands just to the east of the Municipal Building in Manhattan and defiles the approaches to the Brooklyn Bridge is designed to hold nothing but electronic equipment; its windows are mostly dummies, appliqued to a blank surface.

313

314

315

316

317

318, 319   320

321, 322   323

324   325

318. *Africa,* U.S. Custom House
Bowling Green
New York
Daniel Chester French, sculptor
1907

319. *Asia,* U.S. Custom House
Bowling Green
New York
Daniel Chester French, sculptor
1907

320. U.S. Custom House
Bowling Green
New York
Cass Gilbert, architect
1907

321. *Europe,* U.S. Custom House
Bowling Green
New York
Daniel Chester French, sculptor
1907

322. *America,* U.S. Custom
House
Bowling Green
New York
Daniel Chester French, sculptor
1907

323. U.S. Custom House
Bowling Green
New York
Cass Gilbert, architect
1907

324, 325. Office building
375 Pearl Street
New York
Rose, Beaton & Rose,
architects
1978

326. St. Paul's Episcopal Church
58 Third Street
Troy
1828

327. St. Peter's Episcopal Church
151 Genesee Street
Geneva
Richard Upjohn, architect
c. 1858

328. St. Joseph's Church
Ten Broeck Square
Albany
Patrick C. Keeley, architect
1856-60; 1910

329. St. Luke's Church
Route 9
Clermont
Richard Upjohn, architect
c. 1857-59

330. Church
Rome

331. Church
Cedarville

332. First Presbyterian Church
Church Street
Valatie
Ogden & Wright, architects
1878

333. Christ Church
46 River Street
Cooperstown
James Fenimore Cooper,
architect for renovation
1807; renovated 1841

334. Trinity Episcopal Church
Rensselaerville
Ephraim B. Russ, architect
1815

335. Holy Trinity Cathedral
Jordanville
c. 1946-50

The diversity of tongues in New York State (as early as the seventeenth century, eighteen languages were said to be spoken on Manhattan Island alone) has always been matched by a diversity of religions as well. Roman Catholics, Jews, members of the Russian Orthodox Church and innumerable Protestant sects, from Episcopalians, Presbyterians, Baptists, Lutherans, and Methodists to Quakers, Shakers, Mormons, and Christian Scientists, have built their houses of worship throughout the state. These houses range in size from St. John the Divine, in New York City, which is one of the largest cathedrals in the world and may be a century or two away from completion, to tiny chapels that enhance the landscape of upstate New York and yearn every bit as earnestly for God as does St. Patrick's or St. Paul's.

326   327   328

329   330   331

332   333   334

335

336

337

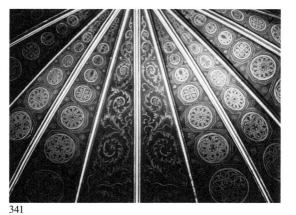

338

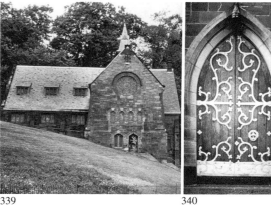

339   340

341

342   343, 344

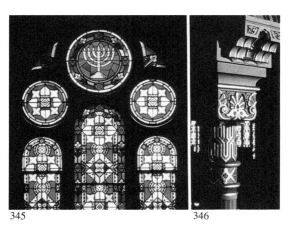

345   346

347

336. East Nassau Baptist Church
East Nassau

337. Christ Episcopal Church
East Main Street
Sackets Harbor
1832

338. Morris Manor Chapel
Route 51
Morris
c. 1870

339. Session House
Woodside Presbyterian Church
Mill and Erie streets
Troy
R.H. Robertson,
architect (attrib.)
1883

340. Woodside Presbyterian
Church
Mill and Erie streets
Troy
Henry Dudley, architect (attrib.)
1868

341. Trinity Episcopal Church
371 Delaware Avenue
Buffalo
Cyrus K. Porter, architect
1886

342-346. Central Synagogue
652 Lexington Avenue
New York
Henry Fernbach, architect
1872

347. St. Paul's Episcopal Church
58 Third Street
Troy
Tiffany Glass & Decoration Co.
(J.A. Holzer), decorators
1891

43

348. The Whaler's Church
Union Street
Sag Harbor
Minard Lafever,
architect (attrib.)
1844

349. Manetto Hill Church
Old Bethpage Village
Old Bethpage
1857

350-352. St. John
the Evangelist Church
Chittenden Road
Stockport
1846

353. Cathedral Church of
St. John the Divine
Amsterdam Avenue at
West 112th Street
New York
Heins & LaFarge, architects;
Cram & Ferguson, architects
begun 1892

354. Christian Church
Bakersville

355. Presbyterian Church
Main Street
Rensselaerville
Ephraim B. Russ, architect
1843

356. St. Patrick's Cathedral
Fifth Avenue between
East 50th and 51st streets
New York
James Renwick, Jr., architect
1858-88

357, 358. St. Paul's Chapel
Broadway between Fulton and
Vesey streets
New York
Thomas McBean, architect;
James Crommelin Lawrence,
architect
1766; 1794

348

349

350

351, 352

353

354

355

356

357

358

Much that we have inherited from the past is of value to us because it is irreplaceable. Workmanship of a high quality was commonplace a century ago; it is far from being commonplace today. Again and again, one sees in some obscure corner of a house or mill or church or barn evidence of a devotion to craft that contemporary life grants little time and few rewards to. The exquisite handiwork of a host of anonymous artisans of long ago not only gives us pleasure but silently urges upon us the possibility that we, too, can accomplish the same ends.

359, 360   361

362, 363   364

365

366

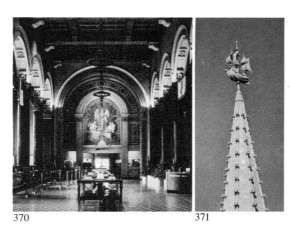

367   368, 369   370   371

359. Sulphur Springs Pavilion
Sharon Springs

360. Campbell-Whittlesey House
123 South Fitzhugh Street
Rochester
1835-36

361. New York State
Department of
Education Building
Washington Avenue
Albany
Henry Hornbostel, architect
1908-12

362. Sylvania
River Road
Barrytown
Charles A. Platt, architect
1905

363. Chapel of the
Good Shepherd
Chautauqua Institution
Chautauqua
c. 1894

364. Rokeby
River Road
Barrytown
1858-59

365. Summerhouse
Genesee Country Museum
Mumford
William Randall, builder;
Simeon Rouse, carver
c. 1828

366, 367. U.S. Custom House
Bowling Green
New York
Cass Gilbert, architect
1907

368. Rochester City Hall
(Federal Building)
Church and
North Fitzhugh streets
Rochester
Harvey Ellis, architect
1885-89

369. Rensselaer County
Courthouse
Second and Congress streets
Troy
M.F. Cummings & Son,
architects
1894-98

370. Rochester Savings Bank
40 Franklin Street
Rochester
McKim, Mead & White with
J. Foster Warner, architects
1928

371. "Half Moon" weathervane
State University of New York
Administrative Headquarters
Albany
Marcus T. Reynolds
1914-18

372. Saratoga Race Track
Union Street
Saratoga Springs

373. Magnesia Springs Pavilion
Sharon Springs
L. Burger, architect
1863

374. Beverwyck
Rensselaer
Frederick Diaper, architect
1839-42

375, 376. New York State
Department of
Education Building
Washington Avenue between
Hawk and Swan streets
Albany
Henry Hornbostel, architect
1908-12

377. Smoking room, Woodside
485 East Avenue
Rochester
Herter Brothers, decorators
c. 1890

378. Mantelpiece
Charles S. Estabrook Estate
Fayetteville
Ward Wellington Ward,
architect;
tile by Henry Mercer
for Moravian
Pottery & Tile Works
1923

379. Roberson Mansion
30 Front Street
Binghamton
C. Edward Vosbury, architect
1904-06

380. Richardson-Bates House
135 East Third Street
Oswego
Andrew Jackson Warner,
architect
1850; 1867; 1883-90

381. U.S. Custom House
Bowling Green
New York
Cass Gilbert, architect
1907

382. Christ Chapel
Trinity Episcopal Church
371 Delaware Avenue
Buffalo
Cram, Goodhue & Ferguson,
architects
1913

383. Roberson Mansion
30 Front Street
Binghamton
C. Edward Vosbury, architect
1904-06

372

373

374

375   376

377   378

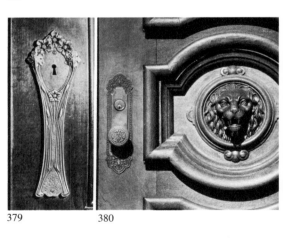

379   380

381   382

383

As the twentieth century draws to a close, we find it harder and harder to discern in the mass-produced homogeneity of contemporary life the varied strands of our architectural heritage. Daily we lose some portion of our astonishing diversity; not a moment too soon, we perceive that we cannot afford to act as our ancestors acted when, without taking thought, they elected again and again to obliterate the past. The Preservation League of New York State and many local organizations are teaching us how to prevent a wanton destruction of the most precious of our structures, whether they be houses, barns, churches, loft buildings, factories, or bridges. Nevertheless, it is a fact that destruction is continuing at a tragic rate. Hundreds of buildings have been lost to us over the past few years.

384. Residence (destroyed)
Troy
c. 1870

385. School 5 (destroyed)
Troy
M.F. Cummings & Son,
architects
c. 1900

386. Hospital
Madison Barracks
Sackets Harbor
c. 1816-19

387. Movie palace (destroyed)
Brooklyn

388. Demolition site
Troy

389. Residence (destroyed)
Troy
c. 1830

384

385   386   387

388

389

390. Irwin-Nally House
Rensselaer
c. 1860

391. Laing Stores (destroyed)
New York
James Bogardus, architect
1848

392. Singer Tower (destroyed)
New York
Ernest Flagg, architect
1907

393. Jerome Mansion
(destroyed)
New York
T.R. Jackson, architect
1859

394. Times Tower (remodeled)
Broadway at West 42nd Street
and Seventh Avenue
New York
Eidlitz & MacKenzie, architects
1904

395, 396. Pennsylvania Station
(destroyed)
New York
McKim, Mead & White,
architects
1910

397. Vassar Cottage
(dismantled)
Springside
Poughkeepsie
Andrew Jackson Downing,
architect
1850-52

398. Ball Academy (destroyed)
Hoosick Falls
1843

390

391

392   393   394

395   396

397   398

As these words are written, many superlative buildings are in jeopardy throughout the state. Thanks to enlightened legislation, some of these buildings will be less difficult to save today than they would have been even a short while ago. Throughout the length and breadth of the state, we have learned much about the sympathetic reuse of old buildings. In scores of towns and cities, Main Streets once threatened with decay and even with abandonment are being given new life. The Jefferson Market Courthouse in New York City has become a branch of the public library. The Federal Archives Building, also in New York City, is currently being turned into apartments, retail shops, and public spaces. The old Rochester Federal Building makes an admirable new city hall. The Delaware and Hudson Railway Company Building, in Albany, has been turned into the administrative headquarters of the State University of New York. One wing of the landmark Villard Houses in New York City has become part of the Helmsley Palace Hotel; another wing serves as The Urban Center, housing the Municipal Art Society and other not-for-profit organizations. The Preservation League itself occupies a nineteenth-century townhouse in Albany.

399. Caretaking complex
Camp Sagamore
near Raquette Lake
begun 1899

400. Sawmill
(destroyed)
Warrensburg

401. Wildmere Hotel
Lake Minnewaska

402. Willard Asylum
for the Chronic Insane
Willard State Psychiatric Center
Willard
1869

399

400

401

402

403. Madison Barracks
Sackets Harbor

404. "The Broadway Approach"
Rensselaer Polytechnic Institute
Troy
Demers & Campaigne,
architects
1907

405. Utica State Hospital
1213 Court Street
Utica
William Clarke, architect
1838-43

406. New York State
Department of
Education Building
Washington Avenue between
Hawk and Swan streets
Albany
Henry Hornbostel, architect
1908-12

407. Cooper-Hewitt Museum
(Andrew Carnegie Mansion)
2 East 91st Street
New York
Babb, Cook & Willard,
architects
1903

408. Camp Sagamore
Sagamore Road
near Raquette Lake
William West Durant, architect
1897

409-411. Federal Archives
Building
641 Washington Street
New York
Willoughby J. Edbrooke,
architect
1899

412-414. Rochester City Hall
(Federal Building)
Church and
North Fitzhugh streets
Rochester
Harvey Ellis, architect
1885-89

403

404

405

406

407

408

409, 410   411

412, 413   414

415

416

417

418 419

420 421 422

423 424

425 426

415. Canfield Casino
Congress Park
Saratoga Springs
1866-69; 1902-03

416. Schlegel Corporation
(Hiram Sibley House)
400 East Avenue
Rochester
1868; 1900

417. Julia Bush Memorial Hall
(First Presbyterian Church)
Russell Sage College
Troy
James Dakin, architect
1836

418, 419. Market Street
Corning

420, 421. Jefferson Market
Library
(Jefferson Market Courthouse)
Sixth Avenue at West 10th Street
New York
Frederick Clarke Withers,
architect
1876

422. Rochester City Hall
(Federal Building)
Church and
North Fitzhugh streets
Rochester
Harvey Ellis, architect
1885-89

423, 424. State University
of New York
Administrative Headquarters
(Delaware and Hudson Railway
Company Building)
Broadway
University Plaza
Albany
Marcus T. Reynolds, architect
1914-18

425, 426. Villard Houses
451-457 Madison Avenue
New York
McKim, Mead & White,
architects
1882-85

427. Church
Clifton Park

428. New York Yacht Club
37 West 44th Street
New York
Warren & Wetmore, architects
1899-1900

429. Portico frieze
Buffalo City Hall
Niagara Square
Buffalo
Albert T. Stewart, sculptor
1929-31

430. Boarding house
Sharon Springs
late 19th century

431. Estabrook Octagon House
9 River Street
Hoosick Falls
Ezra Estabrook, builder
1853-54

432. Edgewood
Alexandria Bay
Thousand Islands

We take as our motto and rallying cry the words of John Ruskin, who in answering the question of whether it was expedient to preserve the buildings of the past, said at once and with passion, *"We have no right whatever to touch them.* They are not ours. They belong partly to those who built them, and partly to all the generations of mankind who are to follow us. . . . It may hereafter be a subject of sorrow, or a cause of injury, to millions, that we have consulted our present convenience when casting down such buildings as we choose to dispense with. That sorrow, that loss we have no right to inflict."

427

428

429

430

431

432

433

434

435

436

437

438

439

440

433. Summerhouse
Genesee Country Museum
Mumford
William Randall, builder;
Simeon Rouse, carver
c. 1828

434. Lawrence J. Fitzgerald
House
39 Tompkins Street
Cortland
1885

435. Yaddo
Union Avenue
Saratoga Springs
William Halsey Wood,
architect
1893

436. Sweetman Barns
Charlton

437. Troy Gas Light Company
Gasholder House
Fifth Avenue and Jefferson
Street
Troy
Frederick A. Sabbaton, engineer
1873

438. Altamont Fairgrounds
Altamont

439. Wilderstein
River Road
Rhinebeck
John Warren Ritch, architect;
Arnout Cannon, Jr., architect;
Calvert Vaux, landscape architect
1853; c. 1880

440. Smith Bly House
4 North Maple Street
Ashville
c. 1835

Preservation League of New York State

Board of Trustees

Anthony N.B. Garvan,
   Chairman
Brendan Gill,
   Chairman Emeritus

Matthew Bender IV
Adriana Scalamandré Bitter
Lawrence Bothwell
Eugenie C. Cowan
David Durst
Daniel W. Gerrity
Roberta Brandes Gratz
Richard Haas
George W. Hamlin IV
Maisie Houghton
Susan Henshaw Jones
Jean R. Knox
Edgar A. Lampert
Jane A. Mallinckrodt
Vera Maxwell
Norman M. Mintz
Elizabeth B. Moynihan
Anthony J. Newman
Richard T. Nicodemus
Donald Oresman
Rev. Thomas F. Pike
Adolf K. Placzek
Samuel P. Reed
Katherine Raub Ridley
Carole Rifkind
David S. Sampson
Paul Segal, AIA
Robert A.M. Stern, FAIA
Lewis A. Swyer
Cynthia C. Wainwright
Tania G. Werbizky
Diana S. Waite,
   Executive Director

Trustees Council

Billie Harrington
Huyler C. Held
John I Mesick
Dorothy M. Miner
Rev. Thomas Phelan
William C. Shopsin, AIA
Carol U. Sisler
Kenneth R. Toole
Barbara F. Van Liew

The Preservation League was founded in 1974 when people who had worked hard to preserve the architectural treasures of their own localities met in a statewide "town meeting." They decided that the best way to help individual communities protect their historic resources was to organize a statewide network of concern and action – a "Preservation League" that would unite and encourage all New Yorkers to safeguard their state's unique architectural heritage.

Through its membership of concerned and active individuals and organizations, the Preservation League serves as a mobilizing force to sound the alert and provide basic assistance to citizens and communities throughout the state. The League provides local groups with the tools and information they need to act more effectively and to meet new threats to our aesthetic and historic past with imaginative community action and with new ideas for the adaptive use of buildings.

Because historic preservation cannot be separated from the complex skein of federal, state, and local regulations, the Preservation League works closely with lawmakers to ensure the best possible climate for preservation activities. Campaigns for the passage of the New York State Historic Preservation Act of 1980 and the Sagamore Land Exchange – the first historic preservation issue ever to appear on the statewide ballot – were spearheaded by the Preservation League.

Of particular concern to the Preservation League are religious properties, once the anchors of every neighborhood, but now the victims of disuse and decay caused by lifestyle and population shifts. Through its Historic Religious Properties Project, the League has issued a primer on basic maintenance procedures, sponsored an awards program, produced a slide/tape program entitled "Stewardship: Responsible Care of Religious Properties," conducted a statewide conference, and provided preservation assistance to congregations and clergy seeking to protect New York's religious architectural heritage.

During the past decade the League has helped more than 250 communities and 410 local groups in all of New York's 62 counties to become effective stewards of our shared past. Through its bimonthly preservation newsletter, technical leaflets and handbooks, workshops and conferences, and film library, the League works to arouse public awareness of the importance of historic preservation. An important part of this effort is the film which accompanies this catalogue. Written and narrated by Brendan Gill, "A Fair Land to Build In: The Architecture of the Empire State" has been broadcast on public television stations throughout New York State and has received numerous screenings by neighborhood and historical organizations, schools, and museums.

For more information on League membership and film rental, contact Preservation League of New York State at 307 Hamilton Street, Albany, New York 12210, telephone 518-462-5658.

Preservation League Publications and Film Rental

How to Care for Religious Properties. Michael F. Lynch. An illustrated, step-by-step guide to architectural stewardship of religious buildings, with guidelines on how to establish a maintenance program, how to conduct a building inspection, and chapters on caring for building materials, decorative features and stained glass, and many other topics. 1982. 40 pp., illus. $1.50.

Preservation for Profit: Ten Case Studies in Commercial Rehabilitation. Cornelia Brooke Gilder. Each illustrated case study includes a history of the project, a description of the rehabilitation work, and financial information. 1980. 28 pp., illus. $3.00.

A Primer: Preservation for the Property Owner. Fifteen articles, prepared by experts, focus on special rehabilitation problems and offer practical, reasonably priced solutions. 1978. 35 pp., illus. $3.00.

In addition to these handbooks, the Preservation League publishes technical leaflets. A complete list of publications is available free of charge. To order publications, send check or money order (less 10 percent discount for Preservation League members) to Preservation League, 307 Hamilton Street, Albany, N.Y. 12210. A discount of 30 percent applies to orders of 10 or more copies of one title, 40 percent to orders of 25 or more copies of one title.

"A Fair Land to Build In: The Architecture of the Empire State" is a 29-minute 16 mm. color film which accompanies this catalogue and which is available for rental from the Preservation League. Written and narrated by Brendan Gill, noted author and drama critic for *The New Yorker*, the film explores the differences in purpose, location, time of construction, building materials, and culture which have converged to produce the state's extraordinary variety of architectural styles. Funding for production of the film was provided by The J. M. Kaplan Fund, the American Express Foundation, the New York State Council on the Arts, Philip Johnson, and anonymous donors.

To rent the film, contact the Preservation League, 307 Hamilton Street, Albany, New York 12210.

Acknowledgements

The Preservation League is grateful to the many individuals who generously lent assistance and advice throughout this project. This project was overseen by Preservation League trustees Brendan Gill, Susan Henshaw Jones, John I Mesick, and William C. Shopsin, and coordinated by Preservation League staff members Frederick D. Cawley and Nancy F. Gerber. Mary Ellen Gadski served as architectural historian. We are indebted to the following individuals for their help: John Winthrop Aldrich, Matthew Bender IV, Mr. and Mrs. Willard C. Bunney, the late Chanler Chapman, Ann ffolliott, Nancy Fogel, Billie Harrington, Kenneth M. Hay, Mrs. Lindsay P. Hilton, Elizabeth G. Holahan, Harvey H. Kaiser, Richard H. Jenrette, Clem Labine, Paul Malo, John S. Margolies, H. Merrill Roenke, Laura Rosen, Ann Webster Smith, Mrs. G. Stanley Smith, Helen A. Wickwire, and Dudley Witney. A special note of thanks is due Mary Ellen Gadski, Christopher Gray, Francis R. Kowsky, Kathleen LaFrank, Paul Malo, John I Mesick, Ann Parks, John G. Waite, and Tania G. Werbizky for reviewing the information presented in the photograph captions.

A Fair Land to Build In: The Architecture of the Empire State has been designed by Chermayeff & Geismar Associates. It was printed on Mohawk Superfine paper by the Rapoport Printing Corporation, using the Stonetone process for the photographs.

Index

Acton Civill Polytechnic Institute, Coeymans, 29
Adler & Sullivan, 23. *See also* Sullivan, Louis
Akin Library, Quaker Hill, 29
Albany, 5, 29, 30, 31, 32, 34, 35, 42, 45, 46, 49, 50, 51
Albany City Hall, 32
Albright-Knox Art Gallery, Buffalo, 28
Albro & Lindeberg, 4
Alexandria Bay, 25, 52
Alfred E. Smith State Office Building, Albany, 5
Allen (Atkinson) House, Rochester, 20, 21
Allen, Augustus Nicholas, 4
Altamont, 53
Altamont Fairgrounds, 53
Alumni Hall, Round Lake, 27
Amagansett, 4
Architectural Iron Works, 36
Argyle, 8
Ashcroft, Geneva, 15
Ashville, 53
Assembly Chamber, New York State Capitol, Albany, 35
Associated Artists, The, 6
Athenaeum Hotel, Chautauqua, 26
Athens, 13
Atkins, Thomas, 16
Atterbury, Grosvenor, 20
Auburn, 12
Aurora, 28, 30

Babb, Cook & Willard, 38, 50
Badger, Alfred M., 13
Badger, Daniel D., 36
Bakersville, 44
Ball Academy, Hoosick Falls, 48
Ballston Spa, 11
Bannerman, Francis, 25
Bannerman's Castle, Pollapel Island, Fishkill, 24, 25
Bannon, L.H., 5
Barnard College, New York, 28
Barnes, Edward Larrabee, 4
Barney, J. Stewart, 29
Baron Steuben Plaza, Corning, 5
Barrytown, 3, 5, 12, 13, 14, 20, 45
Bartholdi, Frédéric Auguste, 11
Bates, William A., 21
Bayard-Condict Building, New York, 38
Bennett, Horace H., 33
Beverwyck, Rensselaer, 46
"Big Duck, The," Riverhead, 6
Binghamton, 46

Blake, Theodore, 25, 26
Bly (Smith) House, Ashville, 53
Bogardus, James, 36, 48
Boldt Castle, Alexandria Bay, 25
Boring & Tilton, 11
Bosworth, William Welles, 5
Bourne Castle, Dark Island, 25
Box Hill, St. James, 18
Bragdon, Claude, 5
Brewster-Burke House, Rochester, 14
Brezee, R. Newton, 11
Brighton, 12
Brighton Township, 25, 26
"Broadway Approach, The," Rensselaer Polytechnic Institute, Troy, 50
Bronx, The, 4, 27
Bronxville, 19, 21
Brooklyn, 4, 47
Brooklyn Bridge, 8, 40
Brown, Timothy, 14
Buffalo, 22, 23, 27, 28, 32, 33, 43, 46, 52
Buffalo City Hall, 33, 52
Buffalo Savings Bank, 22
Buffalo State Hospital, 22
Bunshaft, Gordon, 39
Burden Iron Company, Troy, 10
Burger, L., 24, 46
Burnham, D.H. & Co., 3, 22, 39
Bush (Julia) Memorial Hall, Troy, 51

Campbell-Whittlesey House, Rochester, 5, 13, 45
Camp Pine Knot, Raquette Lake, 25
Camp Sagamore, Raquette Lake, 49, 50
Canaan, 10
Canandaigua, 12
Canfield Casino, Saratoga Springs, 51
Cannon, Arnout, Jr., 53
Cannon Tomb, Oakwood Cemetery, Troy, 4
Carnegie (Andrew) Mansion, New York, 50
Carrère & Hastings, 8, 29
Casa Laura, Lawrence Park, Bronxville, 21
Case Building, Rochester, 11
Cast iron, 36
Cazenovia, 14
Cazenovia Town Offices, 14
Cedarville, 42
Center (Joab) House, Greenport Township, 6
Centerport, 20

Central Synagogue, New York, 43
Chapel of the Good Shepherd, Chautauqua, 45
Charlton, 53
Chautauqua, 26, 45
Chautauqua Institution, 26, 45
Chenango County Courthouse, Norwich, 3
Cherry Island, 25
Childs, 16
Christ Chapel, Trinity Episcopal Church, Buffalo, 46
Christ Church, Cooperstown, 42
Christ Episcopal Church, Sackets Harbor, 43
Christian Church, Bakersville, 44
Chrysler Building, New York, 8, 38, 39
Church, Frederic E., 3, 20
Church Family Meeting House (Second), New Lebanon, 6
Citicorp Center, New York, 39
Clarke, William, 50
Clarksville, 3
Clermont, 42
Clifton Park, 52
Clinton, De Witt, 7
Cobb, William R., 4
Cobblestone Society Museum, Childs, 16
Cobblestone, 16
Coeymans, 12, 29
Coeymans (Ariaanje) House, Coeymans, 12
Coeymans Hollow School, 29
Cohoes, 8, 9, 27
Cohoes Music Hall, 27
Congress Park, Saratoga Springs, 51
Cooper, James Fenimore, 42
Cooper-Hewitt Museum, New York, 50
Cooperstown, 42
Copp (Timothy) House, Sinclairville, 15
Corinth, 13
Corning, 5, 38, 51
Cortland, 18, 53
Coxsackie, 29
Cram & Ferguson, 44
Cram, Goodhue & Ferguson, 46
Croff, Gilbert B., 29
Crouse Memorial College, Syracuse University, Syracuse, 30
Cummings, Marcus F., 27
Cummings & Son, M.F., 30, 33, 38, 45, 47

Dakin, James, 51
Dark Island, 25

Darrow School, New Lebanon, 6
Davis, Alexander Jackson, 12, 14, 15
Delamater House, Rhinebeck, 14
Deland (Henry A.) House, Fairport, 5
Delaware and Hudson Railway
    Company Building, Albany, 49, 51
Demers & Campaigne, 50
Denton (George Washington) House,
    Roslyn, 24
DeVinne Press Building, New York, 38
Diaper, Frederick, 46
Dietel, George J., 33
District 5 Schoolhouse, Childs, 16
Dolge Company Factory, Dolgeville, 9
Dolgeville, 9
Dominy, Nathaniel, V., 6
Downing, Andrew Jackson, 14, 48
Drake (James) Building, Corning, 38
Dudley, Henry, 43
Duke of York (James II), 7
Dunnsville, 12
Durant, William West, 25, 50

East Hampton, 4, 6, 17, 18
East Nassau, 43
East Nassau Baptist Church, 43
East River, 8
Eberson, John, 27
Edbrooke, Willoughby J., 50
Edgewater, Barrytown, 12
Edgewood, Alexandria Bay, 52
"Egg, The," Albany, 34
Eidlitz, Cyrus L.W., 17
Eidlitz, Leopold, 33, 34, 35
Eidlitz & Mackenzie, 48
Eiffel, Gustave, 11
Elbridge, 16
Ellicott Square Building, Buffalo, 22
Ellis, Harvey, 45, 50, 51
Ellis Island, 11
Emma Willard School, Troy, 28, 30
Empire State Building, New York,
    8, 38, 39
Empire State Plaza, Albany, 34
Engle, David H., 8
Erdmann (John E.) House,
    East Hampton, 4
Erie Canal, 7, 8
Estabrook, Ezra, 52
Estabrook (Charles S.) Estate,
    Fayetteville, 46
Estabrook Octagon House,
    Hoosick Falls, 52

Fairport, 5
Fayetteville, 46

Federal Archives Building,
    New York, 49, 50
Federal Building, Rochester, 45, 49,
    50, 51
Fernbach, Henry, 43
Finucane (Richard) House, Rochester, 7
First National Bank, Rochester, 11
First Presbyterian Church, Troy, 51
First Presbyterian Church, Valatie, 42
First Universalist Church, Childs, 16
Fishers Island, 4
Fishkill, 25
Fitzgerald (Lawrence J.) House,
    Cortland, 53
Flagg, Ernest, 48
Flatiron Building, New York, 3, 38, 39
Fonda, 11
Forest Hills, Queens, 20
Forest Hills Gardens, Queens, 20
Fort Hunter, 8
Fort Ticonderoga, 31
Fort Ticonderoga Railroad Station, 31
French, Daniel Chester, 41
French (Hannibal) House, Sag Harbor, 4
Fuller, Thomas, 34
Fulton, 18

Gaines, 6
Gaines Township, 16
Gasholder House, Troy, 53
Gaynor, John P., 37
Genesee Country Museum, Mumford,
    45, 53
Geneseo, 7
Geneva, 13, 15, 42
Georgetown, 14
Gibson, Robert W., 22
Gifford, Aaron, 5
Gifford-Walker House, North Bergen, 5
Gilbert, C.P.H., 19
Gilbert, Cass, 39, 40, 41, 45, 46
Gilbertsville, 4
Glimmerglass State Park, Springfield, 13
Gothic Revival, 14, 15, 17
Gouraud (Jackson) Residence,
    Larchmont, 20
Governor Nelson A. Rockefeller
    Empire State Plaza, Albany, 34
Grand Central Terminal, New York, 31
Granger Homestead, Canandaigua, 12
Great Camps, 25, 26
Great River, 19
Great Western Staircase, New York
    State Capitol, Albany, 34, 35
Greek Revival, 12, 13, 14, 17
Green & Wicks, 22, 28

Greenport Township, 6
Groveland, 31
Groveland Railroad Station, 31
Guaranty Building, Buffalo, 23
Gunther Building, New York, 36
Gurley Company Building, W. & L.E.,
    Troy, 10
Gwathmey-Siegel & Associates, 4

Haight, Charles, 19
Halcott, J.B., 27
Hall of Records, New York, 33
Harmony Manufacturing Company,
    Cohoes, 8, 9
Harrison, Wallace K., 34
Hartford House, Geneseo, 7
Hasbrouck (Abraham) House,
    New Paltz, 12
Haugaard, William, 5
Haughwout Building, New York, 37
Haupt House, Amagansett, 4
Hawks House, Phelps Township, 16
Heins & La Farge, 44
Helmsley-Palace Hotel, New York, 49
Herter Brothers, 3, 46
Hewitt & Hewitt, 25
Highbridge Park, New York, 3
Highbridge Tower, New York, 3
Hiscoe, Charles, 25
Holy Trinity Cathedral, Jordanville, 42
Holzer, J.A., 43
Homer, 14
Hook Windmill, East Hampton, 6
Hooker, Philip, 13
Hoosick Falls, 48, 52
Horgan & Slattery, 33
Hornbostel, Henry, 29, 30, 45, 46, 50
"House of History," Kinderhook, 12
Hudson, Henry, 4
Hunt, Richard Morris, 11
Hyde Hall, Springfield, 13
Hyde Park, 24

Ilium Building, Troy, 38
Indian Castle, 7
Indian Castle Church, 7
Inisfada, North Hills, 20
Irwin-Nally House, Rensselaer, 48
Ithaca, 13

Jackson, T.R., 48
James, Henry, 17
Jefferson Market Courthouse,
    New York, 49, 51
Jefferson Market Library, New York, 51
Jefferson, Thomas, 13

Jerome Mansion, New York, 48
Jervis, John B., 3
Jerusalem, 12
Jewish Museum, The, New York, 19
Johnson, Philip, 4, 6, 39
Jones, Sullivan W., 5, 33
Jordanville, 42

Kamp Kill Kare, Raquette Lake, 25
Keeley, Patrick C., 42
Kellum, John, 33
Kimball, Francis H., 4
Kinderhook, 12
King House, Phelps Township, 16
Kingston/Rondout 2 Lighthouse, 5
Kneses Tifereth Israel Synagogue,
    Port Chester, 6
Kykuit, Pocantico Hills, 8

Lafever, Minard, 44
Laing Stores, New York, 48
Lakeport, 6
Lamb & Rich, 17
Larchmont, 20
Larchmont Shore Club, 20
Latham, O.B., 33
Latham, O.S., 33
Lawrence, James Crommelin, 44
Lawrence Park, Bronxville, 19, 21
Le Brun & Sons, Napoleon, 24
Legislative Reference Library,
    New York State Capitol, Albany, 35
Lever House, New York, 39
Liberty Island, 11
Little Falls, 12
Lockport, 8
Loew's Paradise Theater,
    The Bronx, 27
"Long Island Duckling, The,"
    Riverhead, 4
Lord & Burnham Co., 4
Loudonville, 17
Low (Will H.) House and Studio,
    Lawrence Park, Bronxville, 21
Lyndhurst, Tarrytown, 15
Lyons, 14

McBean, Thomas, 44
McKim, Mead & White, 24, 33, 40,
    45, 48, 51. See also White, Stanford
Madison Barracks, Sackets Harbor,
    47, 50
Magnesia Springs Pavilion,
    Sharon Springs, 24, 46
Major's Inn, Gilbertsville, 4

Manetto Hill Church, Old Bethpage
    Village, 44
Manhattan Bridge, 8
Marcellus, 8
Martin (Darwin D.) House,
    Buffalo, 22
Marymount School, New York, 19
"Mastodon Mill," Cohoes, 8, 9
Melville, Herman, 5
Mercer, Henry, 46
Mies van der Rohe, Ludwig, 39
Mills, Robert, 12
Mohegan Lake, 25
Mohonk Mountain House, New Paltz,
    4, 24
Monroe County Courthouse (Third),
    Rochester, 33
Montauk Club, Brooklyn, 4
Moravian Pottery & Tile Works, 46
Morris, 43
Morris Manor Chapel, Morris, 43
Mount Hope Cemetery, Rochester, 5
Mount Lebanon Shaker Society,
    New Lebanon, 6
Mowbray & Uffinger, 11
Mumford, 45, 53
Municipal Art Society, 49
Municipal Building, New York, 33, 40
Munro House, Elbridge, 16
Munson-Williams-Proctor Institute,
    Utica, 4

Nedrow, 11
Newfield, 14
New Lebanon, 6
New Paltz, 4, 12, 24
New York Botanical Garden,
    The Bronx, 4
New York City, 3, 4, 6, 7, 8, 10, 11, 19,
    22, 28, 29, 30, 31, 33, 36, 37,
    38, 39, 40, 41, 42, 43, 44, 45, 46,
    48, 49, 50, 51, 52
New York Public Library, 29
New York State Capitol, Albany, 34, 35
New York State Department of
    Architecture, 35
New York State Department of
    Education Building, 29, 30, 45, 46,
    50
New York Yacht Club, 52
Niagara Square, Buffalo, 33, 52
Nichols, Charles B., 27
Nichols, O.F., 8
Niskayuna, 8
North Bergen, 5
North Hills, 20

Norwich, 3
Nott Memorial, Union College,
    Schenectady, 30
Number 3 Mill, Cohoes, 8, 9

Oak Hill, 7
Oakwood Cemetery, Troy, 4
Ogden & Wright, 42
Olana, Hudson, 3, 5, 6, 20
Old Bethpage, 44
Old Bethpage Village, 44
Old County Hall, Buffalo, 32
Olmsted Brothers, 20
Onondaga County Courthouse,
    Syracuse, 33
Oswego, 11, 17, 19, 32, 46
Oswego County Courthouse,
    Oswego, 32
Oswego City Hall, 11
Ovid, 33
Oyster Bay, 17

Palmyra, 13
Pennsylvania Station, New York, 48
Performing Arts Center, Albany, 34
Perry, Isaac G., 34, 35
Phelps Township, 16
Pierce & Bickford, 18, 38
"Pink House, The," Wellsville, 15
Platt, Charles, A., 5, 20, 45
Pocantico Hills, 8
Pollapel Island, 25
Pope, John Russell, 25
Port Chester, 6
Porter, Cyrus K., 22, 43
Post, George B., 27
Potter, Edward Tuckerman, 30
Poughkeepsie, 28, 30, 48
Powers Building, Rochester, 37
Presbyterian Church,
    Rensselaerville, 44
Preservation League of New York
    State, 47, 49
Prudential Building, Buffalo, 22, 23

Quackenbush (Schuyler) House,
    East Hampton, 17
Quaker Hill, 29

Randall, William, 45, 53
Rapp, C.W., 27
Rapp, G.W., 27
Raquette Lake, 25, 49, 50 .
Rensselaer, 46, 48
Rensselaer County, 10

Rensselaer County Courthouse,
    Troy, 33, 45
Rensselaer Polytechnic Institute,
    Troy, 50
Rensselaerville, 42, 44
Renwick, James, Jr., 44
Reynolds, Marcus T., 45, 51
Rhinebeck, 14, 53
Richardson, H.H., 22, 32, 34, 35
Richardson-Bates House, Oswego, 17,
    19, 46
Ritch, John Warren, 53
Riverhead, 6
Robertson, R.H., 10, 43
Roberson Mansion, Binghamton, 46
Rochester, 3, 5, 7, 11, 13, 14, 20,
    21, 29, 33, 37, 45, 46, 49, 50, 51
Rochester City Hall, 45, 50, 51
Rochester Free Academy, 29
Rochester Savings Bank, 45
Rodgers, Louis P., 11
Roebling, John A., 8
Roebling, Washington A., 8
Rokeby, Barrytown, 3, 13, 14, 45
Rome, 13, 42
Rondout Creek, 5
Rose, Beaton & Rose, 41
Rose Hill, Geneva, 13
Rose (Henry) House, Jerusalem, 12
Rosetti, A., 29
Roslyn, 24
Roth & Sons, Emery, 8
Round Lake, 27
Rouse, Simeon, 45, 53
Ruskin, John, 52
Russ, Ephraim B., 42, 44
Russell, Archimedes, 30, 33
Russell Sage College, Troy, 51

Sabbaton, Frederick A., 53
Sackets Harbor, 3, 12, 43, 47, 50
Sagamore Hill, Oyster Bay, 17
Sag Harbor, 4, 44
Saint-Gaudens, Augustus, 28
St. James, 18
St. John the Divine, Cathedral Church
    of, New York, 42, 44
St. John the Evangelist Church,
    Stockport, 44
St. Joseph's Church, Albany, 42
St. Luke's Church, Clermont, 42
St. Patrick's Cathedral, New York,
    42, 44
St. Paul's Chapel, New York, 42, 44
St. Paul's Episcopal Cathedral,
    Buffalo, 22

St. Paul's Episcopal Church, Troy,
    42, 43
St. Peter's Episcopal Church,
    Geneva, 42
Salisbury, Orrison, 10
Saratoga Race Track, Saratoga
    Springs, 6, 46
Saratoga Springs, 6, 46, 51, 53
Saunders House, Gaines Township, 16
Schenectady, 30
Schlegel Corporation, Rochester, 51
School 5, Troy, 47
Scott, Walter, 13
Seagram Building, New York, 39
Senate Chamber, New York State
    Capitol, Albany, 34, 35
Seneca County Courthouse, Ovid, 33
Seventh Regiment Armory,
    New York, 6
Sharon Springs, 11, 24, 45, 46, 52
Shea's Buffalo Theater, 27
Shepley, Rutan & Coolidge, 31
Shreve, Lamb & Harmon, 8, 39
Sibley (Hiram) House, Rochester, 51
Silsbee, Joseph Lyman, 11
Sinclairville, 15
Singer Tower, New York, 48
Skidmore, Owings & Merrill, 39
Smith, W. Wheeler, 36
Smith & Yeager, 6
SoHo, New York, 36
Spirit House, Georgetown, 14
Springfield, 13
Springside, Poughkeepsie, 48
Starrett & Van Vleck, 19
State University of New York
    Administrative Headquarters,
    Albany, 45, 49, 51
Station Square, Forest Hills, Queens, 20
Statue of Liberty, 11
Steele, Fletcher, 20, 21
Stem & Fellheimer, 31
Stewart, Albert T., 52
Stockport, 44
Stone, Orringh, 12
Stone-Tolan House, Brighton, 12
Stubbins & Associates, Hugh, 39
Stuyvesant, 14
Stuyvesant Falls, 9
Stuyvesant Falls Mills, 9
Sullivan, Louis, 22, 23, 38
Sulphur Springs Pavilion, Sharon
    Springs, 24, 25
Surrogate's Court, New York, 33
Sweetman Barns, Charlton, 53
Sylvania, Barrytown, 5, 20, 45

Photograph Credits

Syracuse, 11, 30, 31, 33
Syracuse Railroad Station, 31
Syracuse Savings Bank, 11
Syracuse University, 30

Taft, Newell, 14
Taft House, Lyons, 14
Tarrytown, 15
Thomas, Griffith, 36
Thomas, John R., 33
Thomas, J.R., 5
Thomas, Martin & Kirkpatrick, 5
Thousand Islands, 24, 25, 52
"Three Bears, The," Ovid, 33
Tiffany, Louis Comfort, 6
Tiffany Glass & Decoration Co., 43
Times Tower, New York, 48
Topridge, Brighton Township, 25, 26
Trinity Episcopal Church, Buffalo, 43, 46
Trinity Episcopal Church, Rensselaerville, 42
Troy, 4, 10, 13, 14, 27, 28, 29, 30, 33, 38, 42, 43, 45, 47, 50, 51, 53
Troy Gas Light Company, 53
Troy Music Hall, 27
Troy Public Library, 29
Troy Savings Bank, 27
"Turtle House," Greenport Township, 6
Tuxedo Park, 3, 19, 20
Tweed Courthouse, New York, 33

Uncas, Raquette Lake, 25
Union College, Schenectady, 30
Union Mill, Ballston Spa, 11
Union Station, Albany, 30, 31
Union Station, Utica, 31
U. S. Custom House, New York, 40, 41, 45, 46
Untermyer Park, Yonkers, 5
Upjohn, Richard, 22, 42
Urban Center, The, New York, 9
Utica, 3, 4, 31, 50
Utica State Hospital, 50

Valatie, 42
Van Alen, William, 8, 39
Van Auken, D.H., 8, 9
Vanderbilt Mansion, Hyde Park, 24
Vanderbilt Museum and Planetarium, Centerport, 20
Vanderbilt (William K., II) House, Centerport, 20
Vanderburgh, N.R., 11
Vanderpoel (James) House, Kinderhook, 12

Vassar College, Poughkeepsie, 28, 30
Vassar Cottage, Springside, Poughkeepsie, 48
Vaux, Calvert, 3, 15, 20, 53
Verrazano, Giovanni da, 4
Villard Houses, New York, 49, 51
Vosbury, C. Edward, 46

Wade, John J., 33
Wainscott, 26
Warburg (Felix M.) House, New York, 19
Ward, Ward Wellington, 7, 46
Ware, James E., 24
Warner, Andrew Jackson, 5, 17, 19, 29, 32, 37, 46
Warner, J. Foster, 5, 33, 45
Warren & Wetmore, 20, 31, 52
Warrensburg, 49
Waterman, Barnabas, 3, 12
Watervliet, 36
Watervliet Arsenal, 36
Wells College, Aurora, 28, 30
Wellsville, 15
Westbrook, Great River, 19
Whaler's Church, The, Sag Harbor, 44
Whipple House, Gaines Township, 16
White, Horatio Nelson, 11, 32
White, Lawrence Grant, 18
White, Stanford, 3, 6, 18
Whitman, Walt, 5
Wickwire House, Cortland, 18
Wilderstein, Rhinebeck, 53
Wildmere Hotel, Lake Minnewaska, 49
Willard, 49
Willard Asylum for the Chronic Insane, 49
Willard State Psychiatric Center, 49
Windham, 29
Windham Public Library, 29
Windrim, John P., 20
Withers, Frederick Clarke, 51
Wood, William Halsey, 53
Woodside, Rochester, 3, 5, 13, 46
Woodside Presbyterian Church, Troy, 43
Woolworth Building, New York, 38, 39
World Trade Center, New York, 8
Wright, Frank Lloyd, 22, 23

Yaddo, Saratoga Springs, 53
Yamaski & Associates, Minoru, 8
Yonkers, 5
York & Sawyer, 30

(Numbers refer to caption numbers)

Edward Larrabee Barnes, 21
Lynn Beebe, 150, 329
Jack E. Boucher, 121, 125, 133, 440
Sally Brillon, 48, 61
Lynn Canada, 123
Robert E. Charron, 191, 432
College of Architecture, Art and Planning, Cornell University, 117
Dennis Connors, 86
Judy Coyne, 60
Eric Deloney, 77-79, 194
Ed Polk Douglas, 83, 95
Harvey Flad, 439
Bernd Foerster, 3, 71, 226, 334, 398
Friends of Olana, 7, 154
Mary Ellen Gadski, 14, 110, 197
Roger Gerry, 187
Jeffrey Gibbs, 6, 8-11, 22, 25, 27-29, 38, 39, 41, 42, 59, 63-68, 75, 80, 82, 87-91, 96-105, 107-109, 111, 112, 118, 119, 126-132, 134, 138-140, 142, 148, 149, 151, 155, 160, 161, 163, 166-182, 184-186, 203, 204, 206, 208-212, 214-218, 225, 227-229, 231-233, 236, 239, 243-248, 250-257, 260, 263-266, 268-278, 280-286, 295, 326-328, 332, 337-341, 347, 350-352, 359-365, 368-377, 380, 382, 386, 402-406, 412-417, 422-424, 429, 430, 433, 434, 437
Cornelia Brooke Gilder, 32, 51, 122, 241
Larry E. Gobrecht, 23, 114, 221, 222
Gwathmey-Siegel & Associates, 20
Robert Hefner, 12
Historic American Buildings Survey, 288, 290
Johnson/Burgee Architects, 44
Harvey Kaiser, 199
Landmark Society of Western New York, 31, 76
Michael F. Lynch, 30
Paul Malo, 34, 47, 50, 52, 201
Doris Manley, 205, 335, 431
John Margolies, 401
James C. Massey, 69
Mendel · Mesick · Cohen · Waite · Hall Architects, 207
Louise McAllister Merritt, 238
John I Mesick, 81, 106, 124, 234, 349
Norman M. Mintz, 26, 299, 418, 419
Craig Morrison, 213, 387

New York State Department of Commerce, cover, 40, 189, 190, 192
New York State Office of Parks, Recreation and Historic Preservation, 33, 94, 237, 379, 383, 397
New York State Senate, 279
Robert N. Pierpont, 36
Cleota Reed, 45, 378
Laura Rosen, 2, 135, 156-158, 162, 164, 165, 407
Rusty Russell, 1, 4, 17, 43, 53-57, 144-147, 223, 224, 249, 259, 261, 262, 267, 287, 289, 291-294, 298, 300-325, 342-346, 353, 356-358, 366, 367, 381, 409-411, 420, 421, 425, 426, 428
Society for the Preservation of Long Island Antiquities, 141, 153
Susannah Falk Shopsin, 13, 24, 136, 152, 296
Milo V. Stewart, 49, 62, 73, 116, 330, 331, 333
Edward Teitelman, 19, 35, 235, 348, 391, 392, 394
Marcia Toole, 85
Diana S. Waite, 5
John G. Waite, 15, 37, 58, 70, 72, 74, 84, 93, 113, 115, 120, 188, 219, 220, 230, 234, 240, 242, 258, 297, 336, 354, 355, 384, 385, 388-390, 393, 395, 396, 399, 400, 408, 427, 436, 438
Dudley Witney, 16, 46, 137, 143, 159, 183, 193, 195, 196, 198, 200, 202, 435